Vámonos

Mexican Folk Art Transport in English and Spanish

Cynthia Weill

Wooden sculptures from Oaxaca by
**Martín Melchor, Agustín Tinoco Cruz,
Avelino Pérez, and Maximino Santiago**

You can go by tricycle . . .

Puedes ir en triciclo...

by car . . .

en coche...

or with a friend.

o con un amigo o una amiga.

You can go by plane . . .

Puedes ir en avión...

by bike . . .

en bicicleta...

or by bus.

o en autobús.

You can go with your family . . .

Puedes ir con tu familia...

by boat . . .

Barco a la biblioteca

en barco...

or on foot.

o a pie.

You can go by taxi . . .

Puedes ir en taxi...

on a skateboard . . .

en patineta...

or by horse cart.

o en carreta.

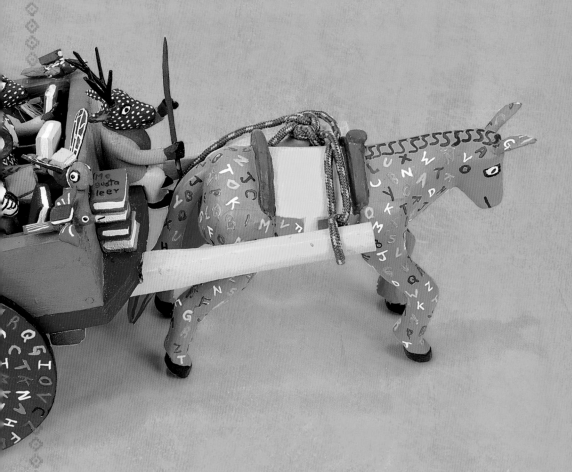

So, how will you get
to the library . . .

¿Entonces, cómo llegarán
a la biblioteca...

dear friends?

**queridas amigas
y queridos amigos?**

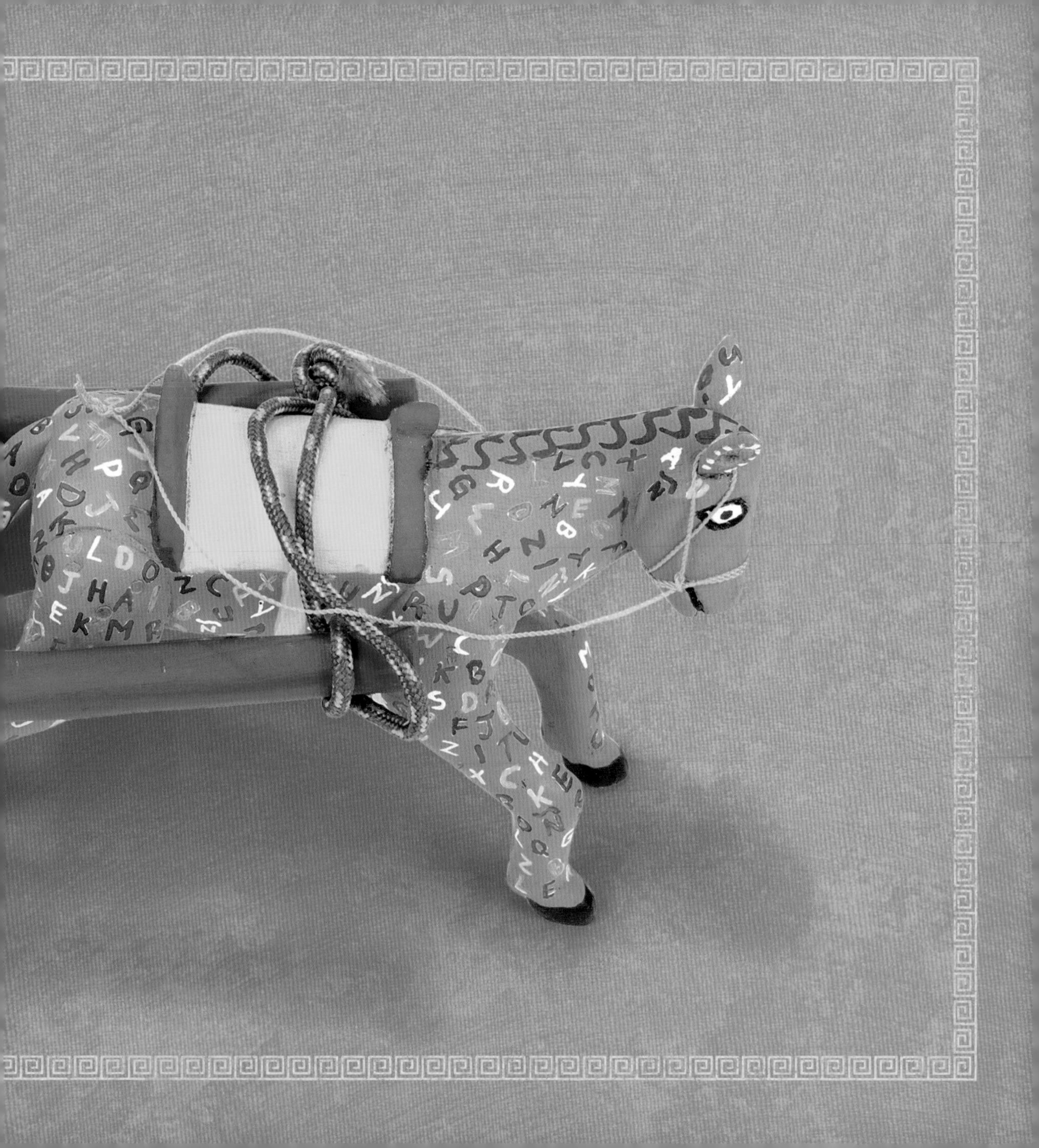

Maximino Santiago   Agustín Tinoco Cruz   Martín Melchor   Avelino Pérez

Richard Keis

The folk-art pieces in *Vámonos* were lovingly handmade by the craftsmen shown above. They are from the state of Oaxaca, Mexico, which is known for its beautiful wood carvings. Agustín, Martín, Maximino, and Avelino are delighted to use their *artesanías* to show their favorite ways to get to the library. For more information, visit cynthiaweill.net.

Dedication

To Bailey and Weill Boucher—no matter how you get there, wishing you a lifetime of wonderful trips to the library.
P.S. I am thrilled to be your auntie.

Very Special Thanks to

Amy Hest, Otto Piron, and Irma, Alejandro, and Panchita of Casa Panchita, Oaxaca.

Thanks to

Jaime Ruiz, Víctor Sánchez, Anne Mayagoitia, Ruth Meyers, Araceli Santiago, Yolanda López Pérez, Hermelinda Ortega, Bacilisa Bautista Jiménez, Amy Mulvihill, Joyce Grossbard, Victoria Weill, and the Bank Street Writers Lab.

Photography by Otto Piron

Cover and Book Design by Sergio Gómez

Text and photographs copyright © 2022 by Cynthia Weill

All rights reserved. No part of this book may be reproduced, transmitted, or stored in an information retrieval system in any form or by any means, electronic, mechanical, photocopying, recording, or otherwise, without written permission from the publisher.

Cinco Puntos Press, an imprint of LEE & LOW BOOKS Inc., 95 Madison Avenue, New York, NY 10016, leeandlow.com

Manufactured in South Korea by Mirae N   First Edition   10 9 8 7 6 5 4 3 2 1

Book production by The Kids at Our House

The text is set in Rockwell Extra Bold and Caslon Pro

ISBN: 978-1-94762-760-4

Cataloging-in-Publication data is on file with the Library of Congress

FSC
www.fsc.org
MIX
Paper from responsible sources
FSC® C010275